FEELINGS GALORE

Sandra Grant-Manderson

Foreword by Heather Royes

FEELINGS GALORE

Copyright © 2018 by Sandra Grant-Manderson

ISBN: 978-1-949343-00-7

DEDICATION

I dedicate this book to my three children; Horace Jnr., Christopher, and Krystal-Kay.

Horace Jnr., and Christopher are now embracing another life, but they inspired and encouraged me to express my feelings in poems. They were very talented, loving and caring sons.

I salute my daughter, Krystal-Kay, who is super talented, and I admire her quest for perfection in all areas of her life.

I love you.

Acknowledgment

I acknowledge and thank the following persons who influenced me in creating this anthology.

My husband, who encouraged me to start writing as an outlet for expressing my feelings. I thank him for the day he said, *"You keep talking to me like you're speaking poetry."* I decided to write them down.

Mr. Allan Lewis, for exposing my poems on the radio. The response to my poems from the public was encouraging.

My father, Charles Prendergast-Grant, who enjoyed listening to my poems and my mother, Valerie, for her warm personality and determination. My gratitude to my siblings and family who have always been a tremendous support to me.

Ms. Aisha-Lee Manderson, my beautiful grand-daughter, for her bubbly personality which kept me living above the sorrows and other challenges I faced.

To Ms. Jennifer Campbell, who typed and listened to my poems.

Much appreciation to Valerie Tate, who transcribed my poems.

I want to thank Crystal Daye, COO of DayeLight Publishers, and her team for the wonderful job they did in bringing this project to life.

Finally, to Heather Royes, who wrote the foreword for this book. Thank you.

FOREWORD

By Heather Royes

This collection of poems is based on the real-life experiences of one woman. Sandra Grant Manderson has used poetry, sometimes written in haste in the bathroom late at night, to get through a life filled with sorrows. There were joys too. But with the tragic deaths of her two grown sons, as well as a fading marital situation, she was forced to continually pull herself through passages that other persons would have found impossible to get over; this included her physical and other challenges due to Multiple Sclerosis.

Sandra does not use clever literary devices nor stress intellectual ruminations. Instead, she often presents the reader with vivid, sometimes, raw vignettes and cameos. Two striking examples are "Wha Dat Fah?", which depicts the murder of her eldest son; *the red blood oozing from the asphalt on the road*, and "Please Don't Cry Mama," which reflects the terror of young children witnessing their mothers suffer. Such dramas unfold as well as moments of happiness that burst through.

Having studied Drama at the Queen's College of the City University of New York, Sandra automatically utilizes this medium to enhance her poetry. "Shackles" and "Black Woman" are dramatic pieces that can be easily transmitted by the Spoken Word or acted out for choral presentations. Even "Service Please" projects scenes from ordinary life in a humanized manner. The art of combining poetry with drama, including daily, domestic drama, makes her collection readable and accessible to many who would not necessarily read poetry.

This is real life, sometimes too harsh for some who cannot face their own demons. It is not for the faint-hearted perhaps, but true to life, and to Sandra, who lays it all out on the table for us.

One of Sandra's favorite poets, Roger McGough, states in his collection "You At the Back", Puffin Books, 1991: *"May your poems act your rage and cry out against the wilderness you have chosen; may they spit blood into the wind."* And that is exactly what Sandra does and does it very well.

Heather Royes, Ph.D.
Kingston, Jamaica
June, 2018

Table of Contents

Section 3

SECTION 1

Performed and

Award-Winning

Poems

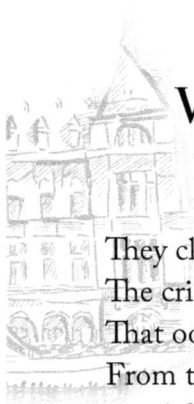

WEH DAT FAH

They cleaned it up
The crimson red blood
That oozed, then slowly drip
From the bullet rigged body that laid
     lifeless on the black tar paved road
That the lumpy blood now caked

A wha dat fah, a whey im do so?
Humans don't have nuh rights again?
Mi can't tell mi story
No jail nuh deh bout or dem too full
While so many lawyers are idle
What is the nation about?
Dead man tell no tales, justice denied
     in every way

A weh him do so?
Thief a phone, pap off man gold chain
     fi cash for gold
Thief a food, im hungry
Maybe im nuh pay the extortionist or
     maybe im see and know too much
And dem already gone wid the gun weh
     wi hear deh pon every scene

They cleaned up the crimson blood
That once caked on the black
    paved road
As the water now pinky red flows
    through the crevasses, over rocks
    and seeping into the cold earth
As it flows to mingle with the gutters of
    life wasted and denied
A wha dat fah, a wha im do so?[1]

---

[1]   Dedicated to my son, Horace Jr.r. (1988-2013)

SHACKLES

Shackles of the past
Are lurking in our hearts and minds
Let us shake those shackles to the ground
For forward must our move be bound

Let us see those shackles for what they are
For only then can we make that start
Shackles that unknowingly we keep
That binds us and holds us at bay
The shackles that our forefathers carried
And now we hold

The shackles that can subtly kill the spirit
And destroy the marrow of our souls
Shackles that unless we know them
Unless we become aware
Will hold us down and will always be there

Let us shake those shackles of ridicule,
    insults
Cowering of our kin
Belittling of each other and negative words
Those shackles were used to keep us at bay
To stop our progress, try what may
Now that we are free
Let us be free indeed

Let us shake those negative vibes
Those shackles of the past
That we ourselves hold, to keep down
    our brother
So, their true worth cannot unfold
As we celebrate our freedom at last
Let us shake off those shackles of the past[2]

---

[2] Performed at the opening of the Literary Competition for the 2009
     Disabled (UN Headquarters) Christ Church, Barbados.

BARK JAMAICA

Ruff, ruff, ruff
Ruff, ruff, ruff
Sounds like barking?
Well – things are tuff
And all I can say when describing
    Jamaica today is ruff, ruff, ruff

Bank rates up today and down
    tomorrow and up again
Mortgage rates suffered the same fate
Businesses are downsizing, and some
    businesses are even capsizing
More unemployment all around
Forgive me if I make the sound
Ruff, ruff, ruff

Taxes on almost everything
High prices everywhere
Our dollar continues to lose ground
Gas prices on a high and the light bill
    can never decline

While nuff food stuff we see and
        cannot buy
University cost going out of reach
Crime is soaring beyond belief
What else must I say when describing
        Jamaica today?
Except – ruff, ruff, ruff, ruff, ruff…[3]

[3]   Performed at the opening of the Literary Competition for the 2009
Disabled (UN Headquarters) Christ Church, Barbados.

PLEASE DON'T CRY MAMA

Please don't cry mama
Please don't cry
We are afraid he will hurt us too,
    that's why
He is coming mama
Don't let him see the pain and anguish
You are showing me

Please don't cry mama
Wash your face and smile
He won't understand, that's why
Don't be mindful of insults hurled
Forget about the shouts, forget about
    the curse
This inner pain, please try to hide
We feel it too mama
But what must we do

We'll try to keep him happy to make
    things better for you

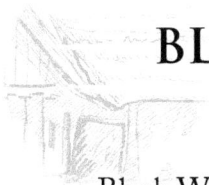

BLACK WOMAN

Black Woman, full of pain
You are strong and have made so
    much gain
But the pain lingers beneath a
    calm exterior
Like the volcanic lava, beneath a serene
    mountain range.

The pain behind your captivating eyes
Your flawless beauty, your
    passionate smile
Belie the volcanic nile inside
The pain that welds like hot lava,
    unable to explode

The pain of childbearing, no?
For that now seems sweet and mellow
Like the good East Indian mango,
    we know
The pain that swells is for the fruits
    we bear,
That gunman, bad man and policeman
    continue to eat away!!

The pain we also carry, the pain of love
    that hurts dearly
When neglected, ill-treated or forlorn
The pain is strong, but we continue to
    carry on
Black woman, full of pain
Black woman, so majestic and strong
Black woman, carry on![4]

---

[4]   Performed at the opening of the PNP Women's Conference in 2013.

BUNGALOW PLEASE

Bwoy, I am getting older
Things are not like they used to be
Can't walk so fast or move up and
    down with effortless ease
Like a steam roller, my movements
    seem curtailed
I am beginning to wonder now
If this is how I am going to remain.

Gone are the days when the stairs were
    a delight
Three, four, five flights, no problem and
    a pleasure for me
Now, one flight up and I can
    hardly breathe
Heaving breast, tightening chest
Cartilage worn and aching swollen knees
Not to mention the challenged muscles,
    singing over seemingly mutilated
    bones, osteo seized.
I don't want to go, not anymore
I can't climb the stairs, like I did before

Step one, pull the other to rest by the
    first foot
Hold the rail like a young suckling
    child, standing in the crib for the
    very first time

Step two, step three
Develop a patient rhythmic stride
Steps that now seem to charter our life
And don't evoke dizziness by looking
    left to right
And be sure to start your upward steps,
    long before sleep visits your eyes,

Aaah! Now at the top, I shuffle to the
    room and my bed with ease
Then my mind regurgitates my
    constant, most urgent plea
Give me a bungalow please!![5]

---
[5]   Performed at the opening of the Literary Competition for the 2009
      Disabled (UN Headquarters) Christ Church, Barbados.

LOVE IS CARE IN ACTION

How can I say, I love you
If I don't show I care
How can I say, I care
If I don't your burdens share

I could share your burden
By understanding your load
I could ease your load
By charities untold

A helping hand
Monetary donations planned
An encouraging word to show
    I understand
Love is care in action[6]

---

6   Performed at the opening of the Literary Competition for the 2009 Disabled (UN Headquarters) Christ Church, Barbados.

MI DEYA

Unoo quiet eh
Yes, shut yuh mouth
Don't talk what yuh know
Or dem wi burn yuh out or dun yuh in
Yuh want get shot or go to jail
Yuh lucky if yuh reach deh, the job
    no done

The state is always right, so no bother
    talk or fight
Yuh too fool
Why unoo have a gun everytime
If them murder yuh
There is a gun on the scene of the crime
    all the time
Whey yuh have it fah and whey yuh get
    it from
We won't know, because yuh no deh
    deh no more

Yuh see how de country a run
No wonder, when yuh ask some man
How yuh do
Him only can smile an sey to yuh,
   "mi deya"[7]

[7]   Performed at Bethel Baptist Church, Jamaica in 2013.

THE TASTE OF FREEDOM

Freedom
Its aroma lingers in the air
Freedom from slavery is mine to keep
No longer will I bow to white supremacy
No longer will its binding brew
Season my being with intoxicating suet

Freedom
Marinated in decades of struggle
Its sauce penetrating, purifying the
        black man's cry

Freedom
Steamed in pain
Fried in agony
Stewed in ongoing struggle for gain

Freedom
A gourmet dish served in slated
        chipped plates
I did partake
But somehow it seems
I am still struggling
With an unfinished meal[8]

---

[8] Received a Certificate of Merit at the 1999 JCDC Literary Arts
     Competition for Adult Poetry.

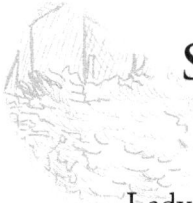

SERVICE PLEASE

Lady at the counter,
Selling services and goods
You know, you are not polite or
    behaving as you should

When I come to purchase
I need attention first
Don't have me waiting while you yap
    on the phone
Even if it's with your beau
I don't care, let him call back or hold

Lady at the counter
Be polite with actions and words
Don't behave as if I disturbed you
Don't roll or cast your eyes, akimbo or
    seem as if to do your work you tire

When I ask you things in English,
    answer in English please
Don't get all expressive and roll out
    dialect or back-yard language at me

Lady at the counter
Times are much too hard
Try to make me feel as if the money
    spent, I can't resist
The goods seem sometimes over priced
But please note that this is true
If you give polite service, I would buy
    the goods from you
To pave the way for my return

Dismiss me with a pleasant smile and
    show that you really care to see
    that I am satisfied[9]

---

[9]   Received a Silver Medal at the 2018 JCDC Literary Arts Competition.

SECTION 2

"Personal

Experiences"

A FATHER BY ANY NAME

Dada, daddy, papa, father, dad
The sound of that name
Could make you happy or sad
Happy, if you have good memories
Of a father that you knew and grew up
　　with too

A man you might not always
　　understand
But often admire the things he'll do
Always busy and hardworking
But does it all for you

A bit stern and hard sometimes
But that's because he cares about your
　　future
Tender when you need him to be
And somehow shows he cares

Provides for your family needs
Willingly able to wipe away your
	doubts and fears
Happy then is the sound of that name
	for you
Dada, daddy, papa, father, dad
Sad, only because you missed the father
	you could have had

Dada, daddy, papa, father, dad

A MOTHER'S CRY

Justice, justice
I need justice
Lady don't cry
Weh justice deh, weh him gone
Im must hear yuh cry an soon answer
    yuh call.

Justice – day and night yuh mother cry
And yuh won't answer her call
What a man hard fi hear
Justice – answer nuh!
Mi tired fi hear the mother shout and
    cry fi yuh

Wait, I hear a rushing sound
Listen, there is hope
Look, at last im deh come

ABUSE

A short word with a cruel twist
Abusive, destructive word that you
    need to miss

Abuse – a looser boomerang
A family's dreams turn to nightmare

Abuse – senseless action, hard to
    understand

Abuse – society's crime catalyst
A child's learning arena

Abuse – like a wife clutching the
    hangman's noose

Abuse!!

BORROWED WOMB

Who spat it in place?
As if I don't know
The seeds of joy or sorrow
Sometimes both
A mixture of misery and pleasure
A pocket of hope of known expectation
    and of unknown outcome

Eagerly awaiting delivery
Months of nurturing,
Days of wonder
Hours of labour
Now giving rise to ceaseless ponder
Seemingly, warranted sacrifices, toil,
    plans and hopes

Nature's curse or blessing?
The price for pleasure
The product of the living crave
The offspring of life
A leased possession
The Eve's curse glorified

My child!
Or am I just a borrowed womb?

DAD

Dad, you are your son's knight in
    shining armor
A role model for him to follow
A daughter's pride and comfort
A guiding light for your children

I need to tell you, so you know
How important you are to us
For I know you always think mother
    gets all the fuss
If only you could spend more time with
    your children
You would realize that fathers have an
    unmatched place
In his children's hearts and lives

The man from whom we got our name
We really need to know
So, we can carry on the name with
    pride and care as we grow
Don't you understand what a father's
    love can do?
Fathers guide and help to pull us
    through the years of frivolous youth
He helps us to focus on the things we
    need to do

Dads help to educate us
So, we can stand on our own
Dads care for us
Provides for us
Guides us
Builds us
Leads us

Oh dad, please note, you hold an
    unmatched place in your children's
    hearts and lives

I love you dad!!

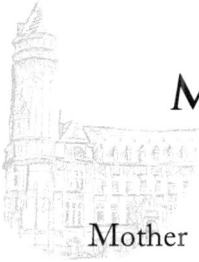

MAMA, MAMA

Mother
Mommy
Mama
Mom
Mi Madre
Ma
However you say it
That name goes so very far
It means a lady full of woes
But she is certainly your friend
Not your foe

An honourable figure that I know
A person to guide you as you grow
A caring hand that understands
A forgiving heart and very smart
A loyal friend to the end
A listening ear that really cares
A gift from God for children

Mother
Mommy
Mama
Mom
Mi Madre
Ma
However you say it
That name goes so very far
Thank God for mothers

MISSING IN ACTION

Im father nuh deya, a mi and the
    pickney one
Im father nuh deya
Im give mi the pickney an gone
A mi wrong fe receive it
An bring it into this world
Im father don't want it
But im had a choice
Im coulda see mi and leave mi alone
Or take precaution that nuh chile no born

Im father no deya, im dead before im born
Badman or police kill im
And leave us to suffer and mourn
Im father nuh deya, im ina prison
Dem sey im commit a crime
Now im leave us without support and
    struggling to survive

Im father nuh deya
But that happen all de time
Im gone, im gone to start another life
    with another woman
Get more children and neglect this child

MY MAN

Warm, gentle, sincere
But certainly, with a no-nonsense air
Ambitious, caring and delightfully
    generous
Businesslike, aggressive yet with a
    charming zest

Fair minded, far sighted and with a
    ferocious zeal
Humourous, witty, fun loving and smooth
Handsome, inner and outer beauty, a
    pleasure to behold
Progressive and proud, understandably so

MY DADDY

My daddy, what a wonderful man
He tried to fulfill the good Lord's plan
Head of his home and family
Guiding his children through the years
Providing for our every need
Working always for our gain
Teaching us the things to help us
    through this life
Like love and commitment
And trying our best at anything we do
Being a good example for us to follow
Taking care of and showing respect to
    our mother
My daddy!
He is the best, I love you daddy.

MOTHER'S LAMENT

How have I failed you my child
Was it my weak character
Was it my passive state
How have I failed you my child
Were you born in the wrong home, did
     I set the wrong tone

How I have failed you my child
I made the wrong man your dad, now
     we are all sad
I have failed you my child
My own bitterness and pain made me
     not attend to your needs

Why did I not answer your cry
Your shouts for guidance, discipline,
     unconditional love and
     understanding.
What have I done, why didn't I see
Will you ever forgive me?

MISSING YOU

The passion of love
Rides my being
When you are not here with me
The thoughts of your love
Keeps me going

Though days seem long and lonely
The meaning of love
Filtrates my understanding
As endless thoughts of you consume me

The working of love is no labour
For our love is a treasured pleasure
The battles of love (easily forgotten)
Finds surrender and boundless
    forgiveness

BEING JUST ME

I am not your child
Don't tell me what to wear
Don't tell me how to speak
Don't tell me how to walk or run
Don't tell me how to plan my time,
And please don't give me that
    disapproving eye

For now I realize the final goal it leads to
I want to let you know
How inside me anger flows
Pleasing you alone and not destroying me
For I feel I am robbed of being me
The me that yearns for expression of
    some sort
In how I speak or how I walk

Yes, I try to do things your way
But inside please note
I am dying each day
For I am no longer sure
Of what is right to do
I feel unsure of my every move
And somehow await your correcting word

The final blow to my hidden ego
Then I am left hungry
Hungry for the sound of any voice with
    an approving word
To take me back down to earth
Where I can feel the real me
And walk with my head up high and
    be assured
Yes, I am someone of worth

WHAT IS THERE TO LOVE

Shouts and insults
That is all
No emotional support
It's a problem
I need someone who cares

No hugs, no kisses, no passing smiles
No greeting, no hello
No show of love
The kids are baffled
Why I am still here

Love that has died
A natural death
I have not chosen
To come to grips with yet

Do I love him?
Need to ask myself why
I need to ask my self
What is there to love?

ANNIVERSARY PLEA

Give me back what you stole from me
Give me back what I feel you did steal
Give me back something I always need
Please give me back your tender love
    and my dignity

Years of scoff it now seems
Have taken an unfair toll on me
Years of pain of insults hurled
Have finally made me lose my worth

Years of feeling that I am no good
Cause me not to behave as I should
Please take no more, that is my plea
Start giving me back
What you took from me

Help me to feel loved and needed
    my dear
Don't always throw insults and
    criticisms so clear
My children, I feel, are disregarding me
Yes, it's their pity alone I see

Give me back, I won't lose any more
Give me back what I had before
Once with pleasure so clearly I see
Your approving look when you smiled
     at me

I felt somehow the world was mine
I soared upon the clouds so high
Your loving touch, your tender kiss
Words of endearment you once would say
Made me feel sure you held me dear

For this Anniversary darling
When nuptial vows celebrating their
     binding tease
This alone remains my plea
Give me back what you took from me

A WIFE'S WISH

If only I could please you my love
If there was something I did right
I used to be able to, but now it seems
I am not the one to fulfill your dreams
Nor share your life

Oh, if only I could recapture
Some of those early days
When you watched what you did
And cared what you say
The days not long after we said I do
Those days I think I was precious to you
But now it seems
I am no longer your love and friend
No caring words
Or words of encouragement
Just a long list of things you do not
        approve
Never able to please you
No matter what my move
Yes, I washed the dishes
But the floor is not clean
The food not ready on time
The kids not looked after well

Yet it seems, I give them so much of
    my time
And then, I say too many unnecessary
    words
That sometimes boggles your mind
I wish I felt I could do something right

Oh, if only we could recapture the days
When you were my lover, my darling,
    my friend

A WIFE'S PLEA

Respect my emotions
For they are mine and comprised to meet
Specific needs in me

Respect my likes and dislikes
Because they are a part of me
That has been molded in me from
    my youth

Try to understand my sensitivity
For my thinking is different from yours
Allow me space for self-development
For no one wants to remain stagnant

Remember our need to remain individuals
For our lives is not a merger, but a
    sharing
Sharing in each other's goals,
    aspirations, desires and needs

TRIBUTE TO MOTHER

Oh Mom, I wish I told you long ago
How much you mean to me
But I didn't really understand
Until I became a mom you see

Now I know how much you did
And what you gave up for me
Your freedom, your time, your comfort
And all your childhood dreams
For I became the main reason
You struggled on each day
No matter how you felt
Or what may come your way

Through hard work or play
Whatever the day,
Your goal and focus never sway
My comfort, my well-being, my
    daily bread
And somewhere always to lay my head

A good father you chose for me
To help you with my care
Although I know, you would carry on
Even if he wasn't there

Now I am grown
I want to give you all the honour and
    thanks you deserve
For you have given me your time, your
    youth, your care
And your love

I love you mom!

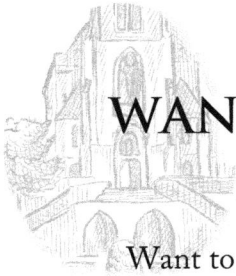

WANT TO BE CLOSER

Want to be closer, but how can that be?
For you are too busy seeing through me
No conversations about you and me
    doing things together
Or sharing our plans and hopes for
    future days

Too busy seeing what I should have done,
    could have done or ought to do
Instead of planning our could be moves
You are too busy criticizing what I
    should do did or have done

I want to please you some, but I am
    distraught by my constant failure
    of things I did and things to come
You see through me too much my dear
The mara genie glass of your eyes makes
    my pathway much too clear

I see hopes of failure, that's for sure
Because I have never pleased you before
I often hoped that I could someday you
    please
But already, you have sentenced me

WAS THIS HE

Where is the man I married?
Has life ills done him in
Has misery engulfed his being?
Has time removed his shinning
    breast plate
Of passion and kindness
Is his helmet of hope rusted beyond repair?

I go in search of him
I plunge on through the maze
The unclear path with no clear marks
I plunge on through the maze, its
    prickly edges constantly to avoid

I hope to behold my love of old
My knight I adore

Where is the man I married?
Was this he?
Camouflaged in the passion of love
Hidden in the heat of desire
Submerged in the quest for gainful
    impressions
Covered in the blanket of lust
Armed with the sword to conquer

Now alas, a clear path I see
I look, it reveals
My knight in shining armour
Now stands naked before me

SECTION 3

Social Issues

BLACK MAN

Black man, do you know
Black man, do you know
Black man, do you hear
Black man, do you see
Black man, do you care

Years of freedom have come your way
Decades of being nobody's slave
Years of climbing to the top
Struggling, ploughing the path to clear

Black man, listen and you will hear
The drums of freedom echoing still
Calling for your superior will
Black man look, the cloud of doubts
      are thinning
The fog of inhibitions is clearing your path

Black man, see a colour prejudice world
      aside to cast
Black man, do you care about the past
Is it embedded in your mind?
The struggles we have conquered at last.

MISSING DAD

Daddy, daddy
Where ever you are
        I hope somehow you know
How often I think of you and that I
        miss you so

Mother is great
I need her, and I am so glad she is here
But daddy, please note that I need you too
And need to know you care,

At this time of year, when I see other
        fathers around
I really wish I knew where my father
        could be found
And so, I close my eyes and think that
        you are somewhere well and fine
And praying, dear Lord, bless those
        children of mine
Help me to find my way back to them
That they will somehow know that I
        really love them and miss them so

But daddy, please forgive me
If often my hope sways
For I am growing up really quick and I
    need my father today!

PICKNEY WOES

Mama, mama you don't love me
Yuh nuh love me still
Not because yuh now hate daddy
A mi yuh want fi kill

Yuh sey im no good, im no good
An me look like im nuff
But a nuh mi lick yuh mama
A nuh mi lick yuh, true?

If yuh did listen to mi and don't tell im
    all the bad things mi duh
Mi neva finish mi homework, neva wan
    go a school this morning
Eat off all the lunch money mi get fi
    de week
Im wouldn't quarrel with mi an cuss yuh
Unoo just want an excuse fi treat mi bad
An tek out yuh frustration pon mi.

Mi did tell yuh
No open yuh mouth and tell im
    everything mi duh
Because a nuh only yuh im a go lick
Im a go lick mi too

DEEP WITHIN ME

There is a stranger surfacing without at
    my call
The stranger long hidden in me
With my feelings held deep within
This stranger that seems unknown
Formerly lived within me
Carefree,
Happy,
Loving,
Confident and alive

This stranger I knew before,
And once again she'll be a part of me
Re-igniting some happiness in me,
Pushing aside the stone of ego pains
Helping me find relief from this alter ego

SHATTERED LIVES

What's the fight?
What's the aim?
Where shall it lead to?
What's the game?
What do you want?
What do I need?
Can need and desire intertwine
To produce the outcome necessary to
    call a truce?

How willing are you?
How willing am I
To work out things
Shall we try?
Shall hurt continue
Are things benign?
What path shall we take?
The pendulum is swinging faster
The symphony is losing its melody
Crescendo

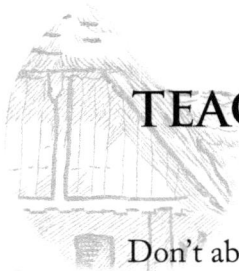

TEACHER TEACHER

Don't abuse me with your words
I am here to learn
You are here to do a job and earn
Your abusive attitude and words
Bring out the worst in me sometimes
And impairs my capacity to grasp
The important things you are trying
    to teach

Don't tell me I am dumb
Even when I don't seem to understand
What you have taught

Don't say I am stupid or fool
Because that's not nice and it is not true

DON'T BURY ME
IN THE KITCHEN

Don't bury me in the kitchen
That's not where I want to be
Among the pots and pans and dishes
That's not the place for me

Don't leave me in the kitchen
Please, I must be free
I need to have some fun
To run or play hide and seek

The dirty pots from yesterday are still
        looking at me
And the one that cooked the red peas
        soup
Has a strong odor throwing at me
Please don't bury me in the kitchen
You know that's not my place

I am among the talented people
And I have a pretty face

www.ingramcontent.com/pod-product-compliance
Lightning Source LLC
LaVergne TN
LVHW051816080426
835513LV00017B/1983